MARCEL GRANDJANY

Aria in Classic Style

for Harp and Organ

This composition is also published for
harp and string orchestra
(*See AMP Catalogue of Orchestra Music*)

Associated Music Publishers, Inc.

DISTRIBUTED BY

HAL•LEONARD®
CORPORATION

7777 W. BLUEMOUND RD. P.O. BOX 13819 MILWAUKEE, WI 53213

TO MRS. ELIZABETH SPRAGUE COOLIDGE

ARIA IN CLASSIC STYLE
for Harp and Organ

MARCEL GRANDJANY

SCORE

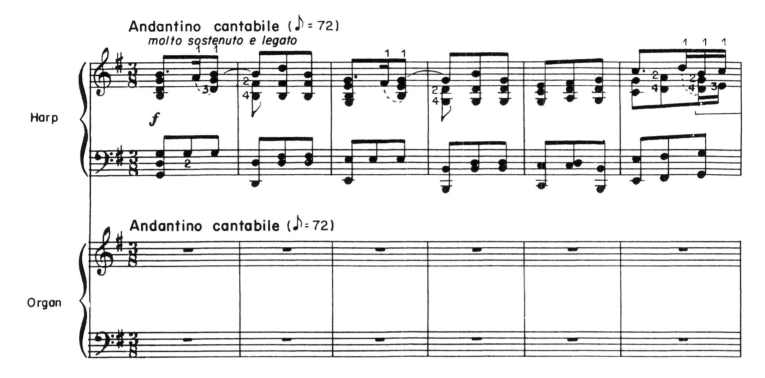

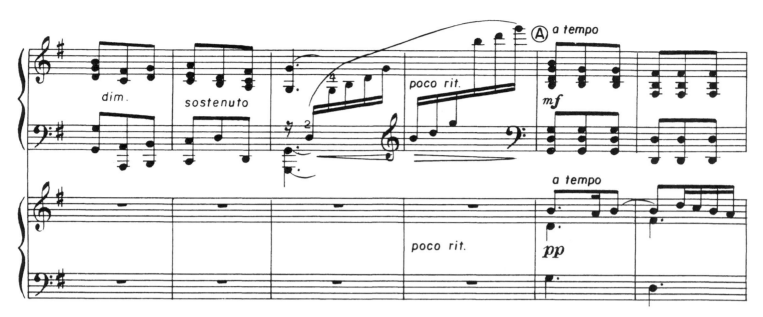

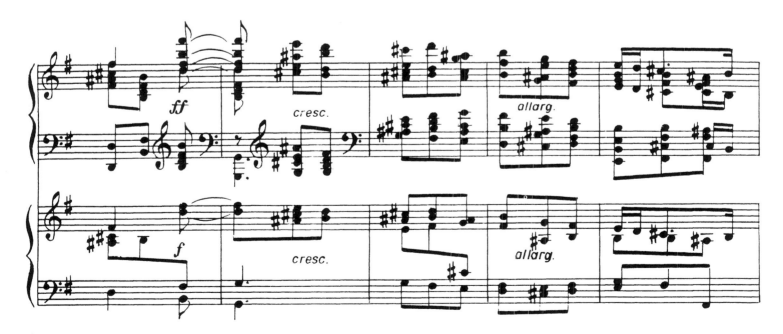

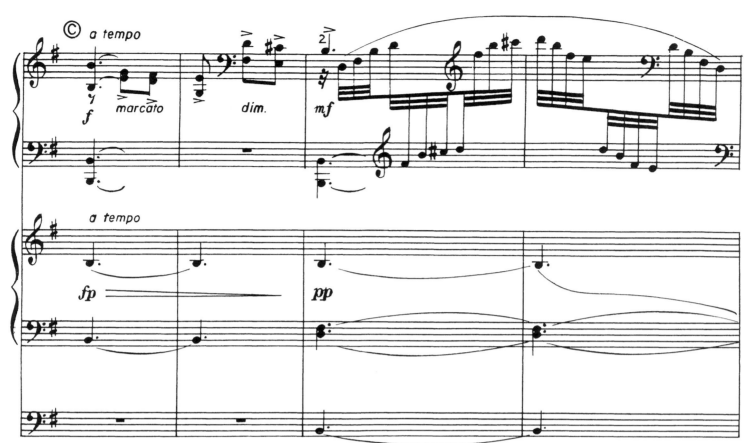

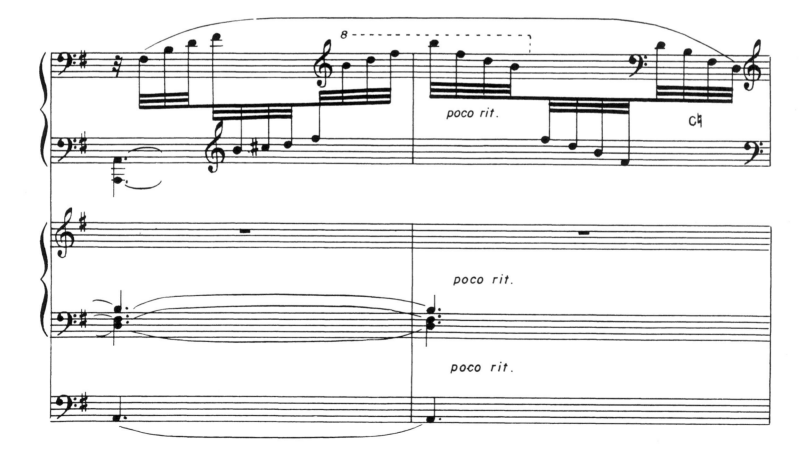

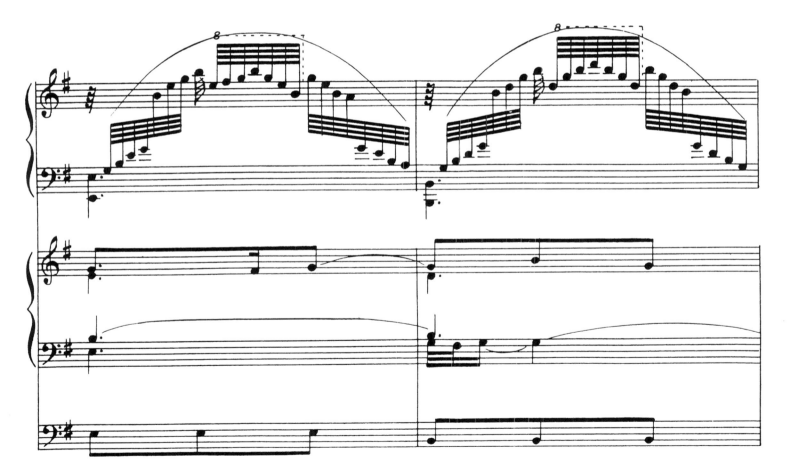

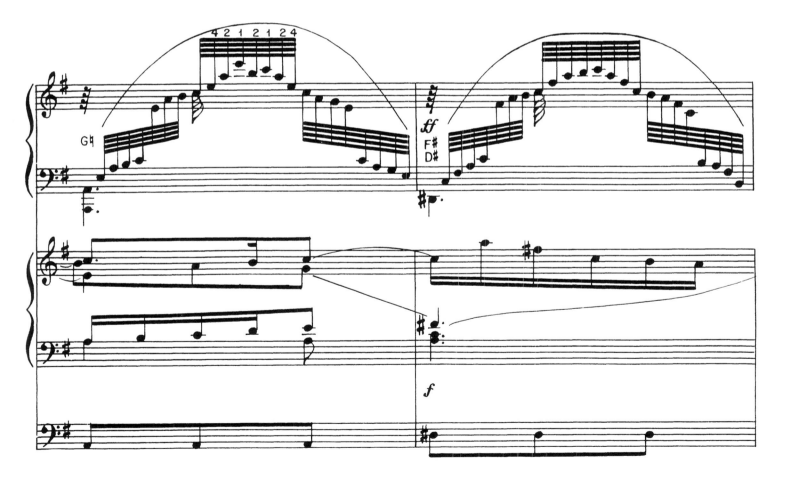

ARIA IN CLASSIC STYLE
for Harp and Organ

MARCEL GRANDJANY

Harp

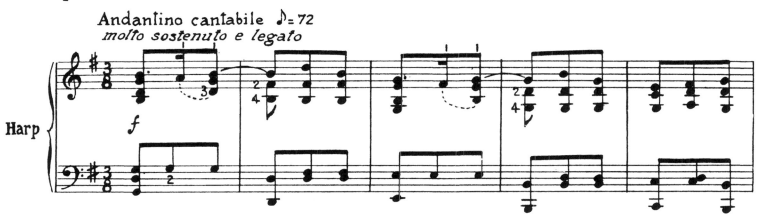

Harp

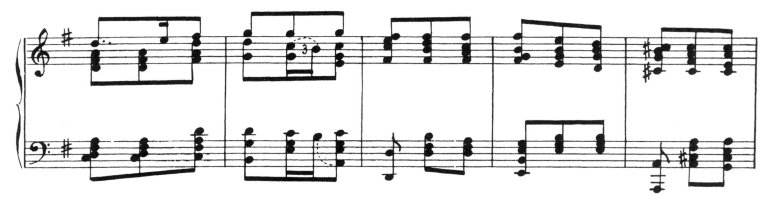

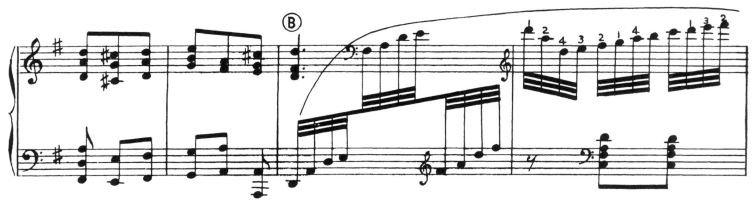

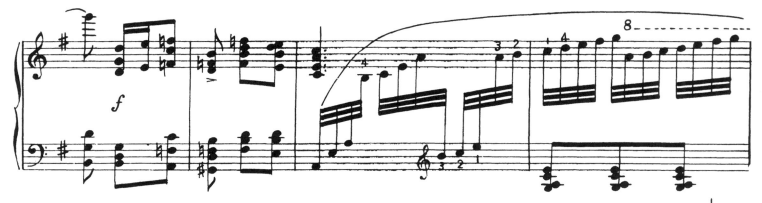

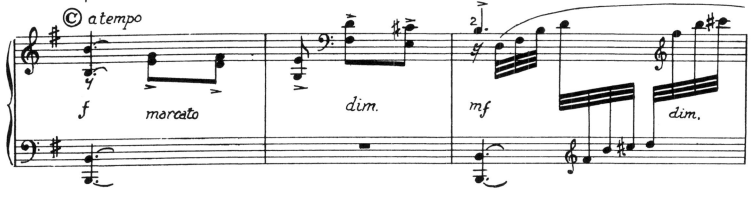

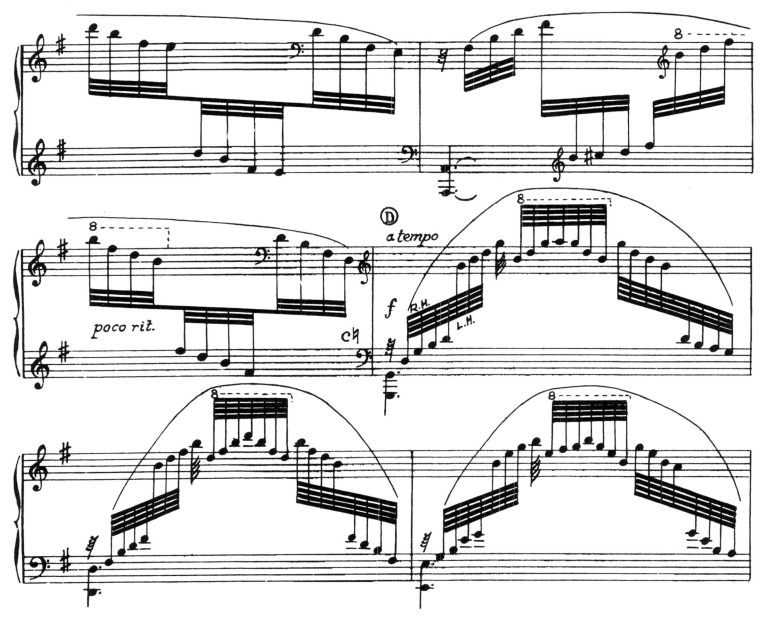

Harp

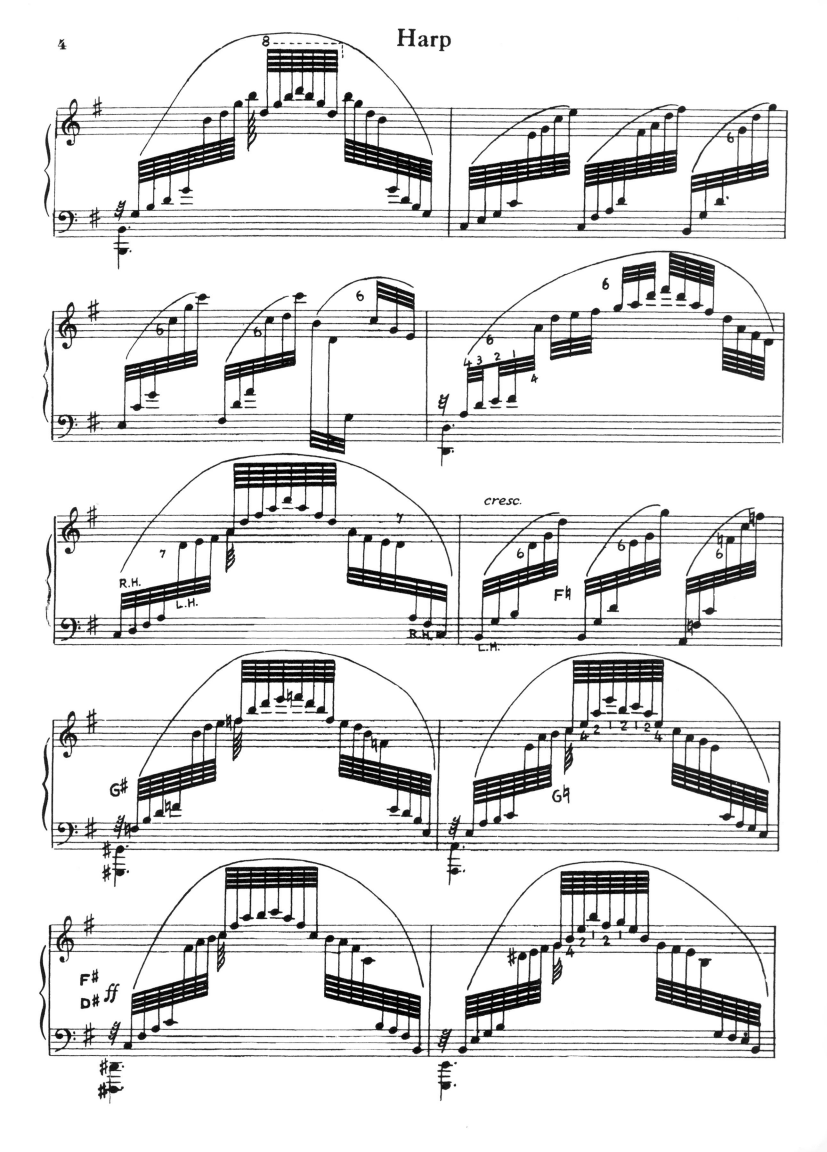

Harp

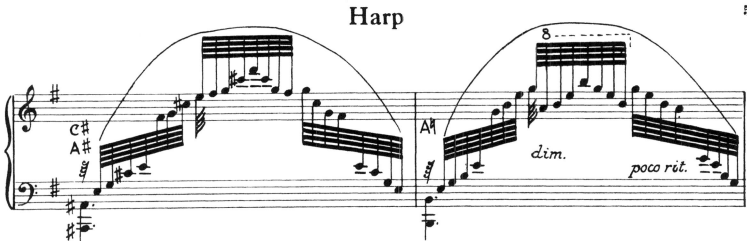

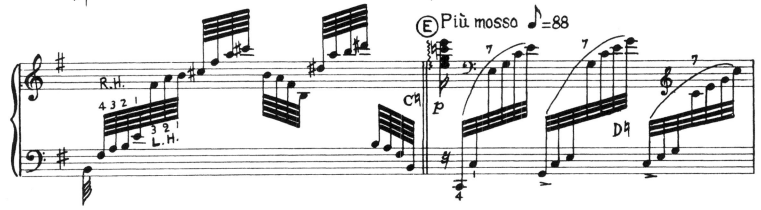

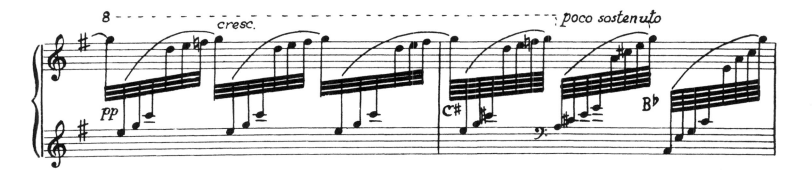

Harp

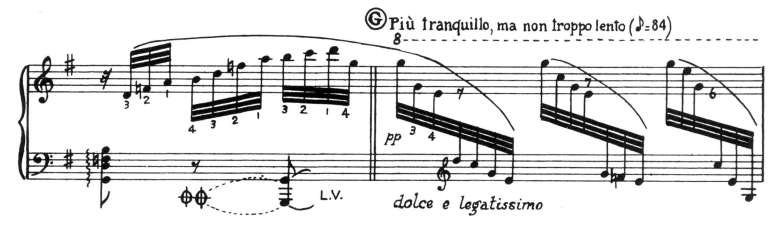

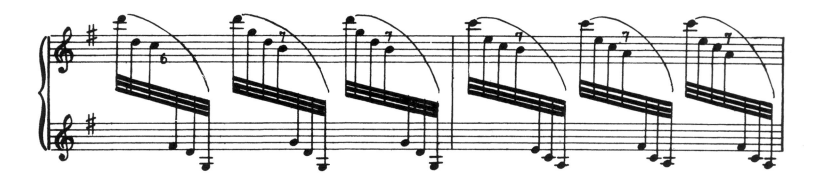

Harp

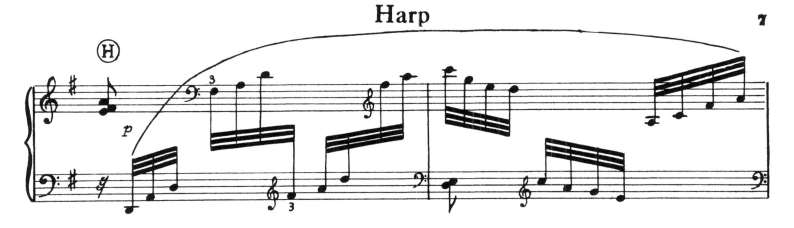

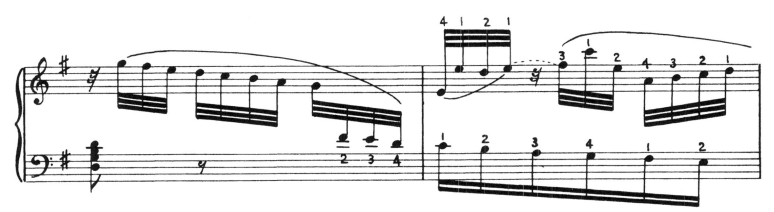

cresc. e stringendo poco a poco

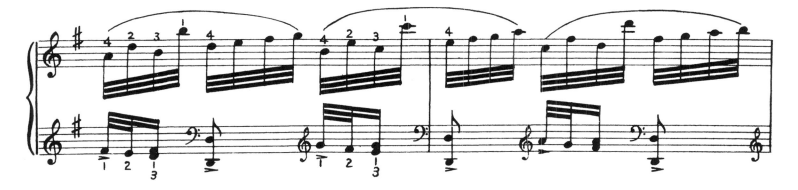

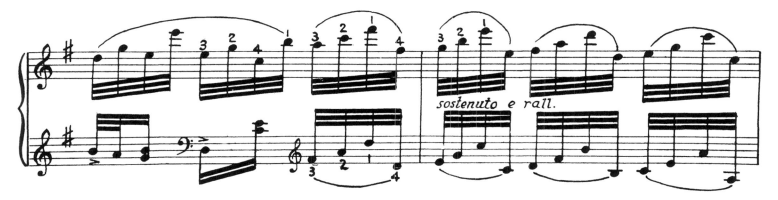

sostenuto e rall.

Harp

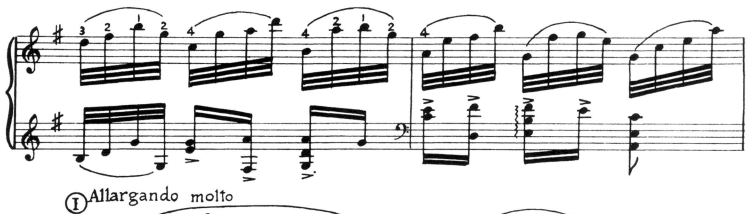

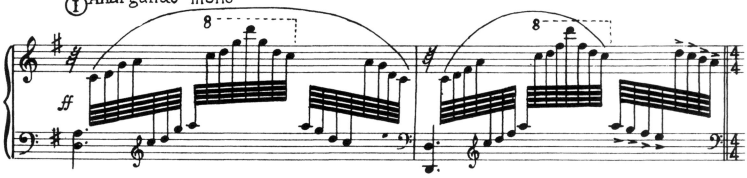

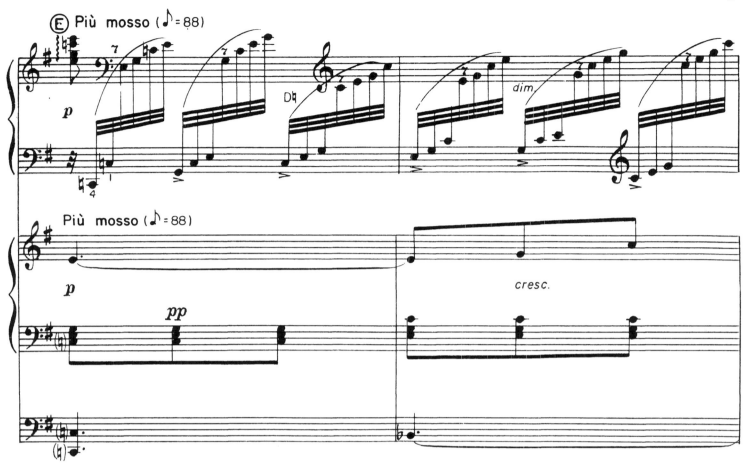

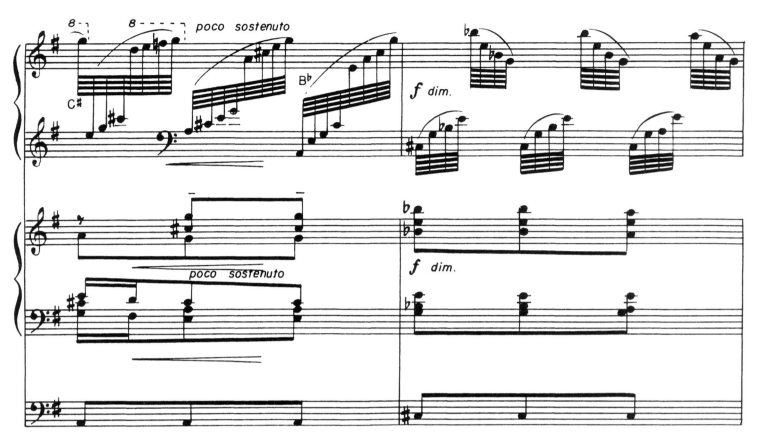

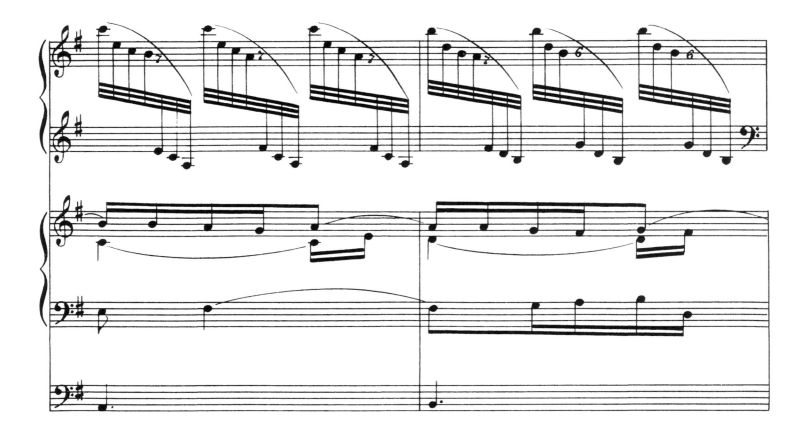

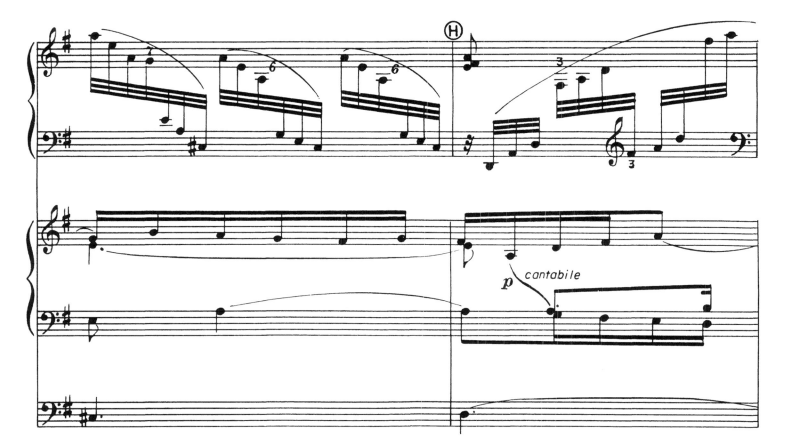

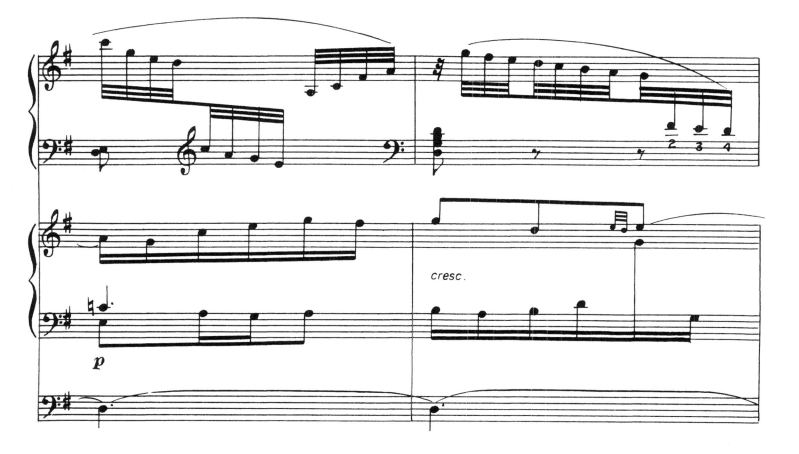

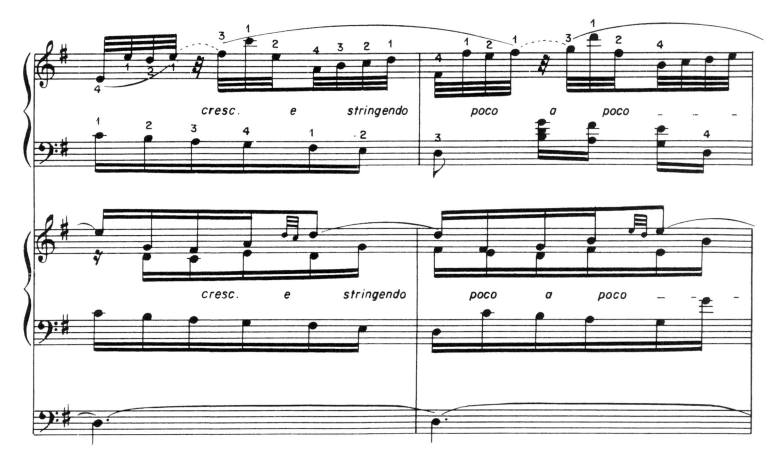

cresc. e stringendo poco a poco

cresc. e stringendo poco a poco

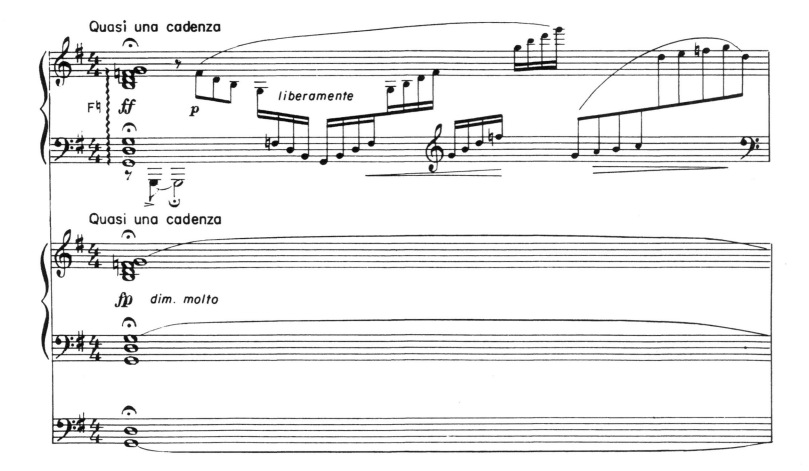

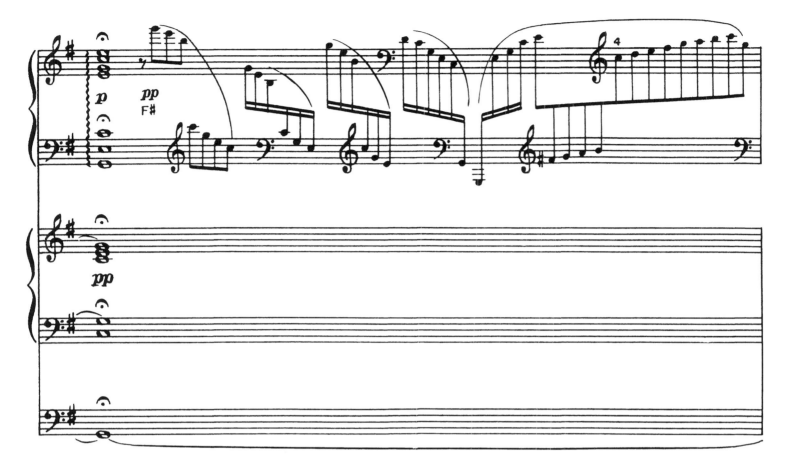

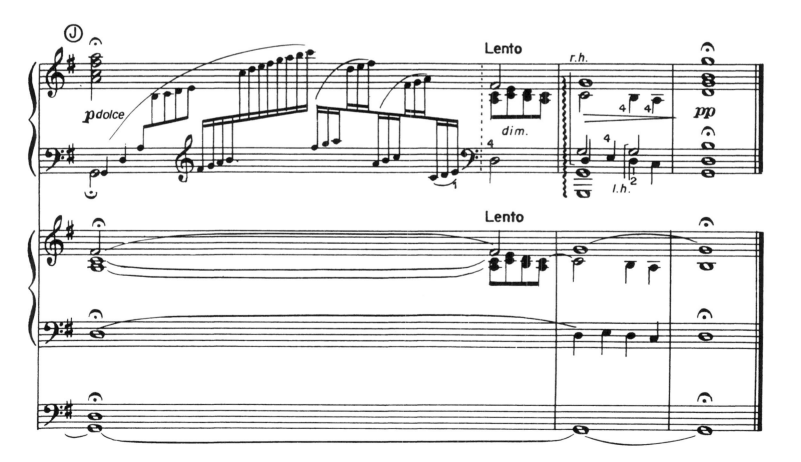